Learn with Me: Math Basics

Carson-Dellosa Publishing LLC
Greensboro, North Carolina

Note that some activities in this book may present safety issues. Before beginning the activities, ask families' permission and inquire about the following:

- Children's food allergies and religious or other food restrictions
- Possible latex allergies
- Children's scent sensitivities and/or allergies
- Children's plant and animal allergies

Also, remember:

- Uninflated or popped balloons may present a choking hazard.
- Magnets and small pieces containing magnets should be kept away from young children who might mistakenly or intentionally swallow them. Seek immediate medical attention if you suspect a child may have swallowed a magnet.
- Exercise activities may require adult supervision. Children should always warm up prior to beginning any exercise activity and should stop immediately if they feel any discomfort during exercise.
- All children's families are different. Before beginning any family activity, review the activity cards and remove any that could cause sensitivity issues.

Credits

Content Editor: Joanie Oliphant

Copy Editor: Jesse Koziol

Layout Design: Lori Jackson

Spectrum
An imprint of Carson-Dellosa Publishing LLC
PO Box 35665
Greensboro, NC 27425 USA
www.carsondellosa.com

ISBN 978-1-936024-74-2
02-210147811

Table of Contents

Dear Family Member,

Welcome to *Learn with Me: Math Basics*. You and your child are about to start on a new learning adventure. Recent research tells us that the first five years of life are a period of rapid growth in all areas of your child's development. It is in these years that children develop the basic knowledge, understanding, and interests they need to reach the goal of being successful learners.

Learn with Me: Math Basics is for families whose children have not yet been to kindergarten. Whether or not your child has attended an early childhood program, kindergarten will be a big change in your child's life. Each day your child learns through play. Perhaps you have observed your child sorting interlocking blocks by color or size. Maybe your child has experimented with shapes by drawing circles or moons on the sidewalk with chalk. Your child is naturally building math skills and learning new concepts through play. By working together on the activities in this book, you will be helping your child learn more about important mathematics concepts.

This book includes activities that involve counting, recognizing and matching shapes, working with patterns, and problem solving. Because fine motor development is also important, the tasks involve cutting with scissors, coloring, and gluing. Objects and shapes with dotted lines are to be cut out. Encourage your child to use the activities to practice these important fine motor skills, but adjust the activities to meet your child's individual needs. The directions are written for you to read to your child. When necessary, change the wording to match the activity to your child's needs and interests.

This is a "togetherness" book. Each activity is meant for adults and children to work on together. As you work together on the activities in this book, focus on having fun and on the excitement your child feels upon mastering new skills. Children naturally enjoy practicing skills over and over again. The majority of the activities are designed to use more than once. We encourage you to plan ahead for this by preparing a box, such as a shirt box, to store the games. Write your child's name on the box and decorate it together. Use resealable plastic bags to store the game cards, puzzle pieces, and patterns. If your child seems to especially enjoy a particular activity, consider laminating it for strength. As a family, there is nothing better you can do to ensure your child's educational success than to spend time together. Enjoy your *Learn with Me: Math Basics* adventure!

Enjoy learning together!

The Spectrum Team

Two-Piece Number Puzzles

This activity is more like puzzle play than math practice! It is a self-checking activity that will let your child know right away when his answers are correct. Create the puzzle game for numbers 0 to 5 using the patterns and directions provided on page 7. Later, when your child is ready to learn the numbers 6 to 10, make a two-piece puzzle for each number on index cards or pieces of cardboard. On the left side of each card, put stickers to represent the number you have written on the right side. Cut the cards in two, varying the design of each cut so that there is only one correct fit. Two-piece puzzles are also effective for matching uppercase and lowercase letters, color words to colors, and photographs of family members to their names. The possibilities are endless.

File Folder Game

File folder games can be fun and educational. For this activity, cut out the barns on page 7 and tape them to a snack-size resealable plastic bag. (See illustration.) Label each barn with a number. Tape the bags to a file folder, leaving the top open so that animals may be put into the barn. Use farm animal stickers or farm animal foam shapes to make animals for the barn. Place stickers on heavy paper (the top of a shirt box works well) and cut them out. Prepare many animals. The goal for your child is to identify the number on each barn and place the correct number of animals in the corresponding bag.

Make other file folder games using paper flowers and insect stickers, paper trees and apple stickers, or other fun combinations. Inexpensive foam shapes are available at discount stores and make wonderful pieces for file folder games.

Number Jumping

This is a great rainy-day activity when your child needs active movement but cannot go outside. You will need an old plastic tablecloth with no designs. Using a permanent black marker, draw a path, a hopscotch grid, or a pond with stones on the tablecloth. Label each section with a number. Have your child jump on the numbers in sequence, counting forward or counting backward. Alternately, just have her jump on any number and say the name of that number out loud. This activity is also fun to do with beanbags. Have her throw the beanbag and then tell you what number it lands on.

Shirt Box Counting

Make a counting board on the inside bottom of a shirt box. (See illustration.) Make corresponding number cards from index cards. Have your child count the dots in each square and place the matching number card on top of that square. When your child is finished, simply put the number cards back in the box, put on the cover, and store for use on another day.

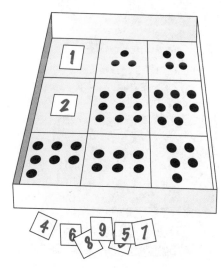

Artistic Shapes

There are many ways for you and your child to make shapes that will allow your child to touch and feel the actual forms. Multisensory learning (using more than one of the five senses at a time) can be a powerful teaching tool for a young child. Not only is the child able to see the shape and verbally identify it, but he can also recognize the shape by the way it feels. Here are some fun ideas for creating touchable shapes.

- **Play Dough Shapes:** Roll play dough into a flat pancake. Have fun changing the pancake to form different shapes.
- **Dot-to-Dot Shapes:** Make a dot-to-dot shape on a sheet of paper. Instead of using a pencil, have your child use white glue or glitter glue that dries raised to connect the dots. When the glue is dry, have him trace a finger over the solid glue to feel the shape.
- **Yarn Pictures:** Dip pieces of colored yarn in white glue. Arrange the yarn in shapes on a sheet of construction paper. When the glue is dry, your child can feel the shape by touching the yarn.
- **Shape Collage:** Using a variety of colors of construction paper, precut several paper shapes. Let your child create a collage by gluing the shapes onto a large sheet of construction paper.

Fishing for Shapes

Children love to "fish" with magnets. Make a simple fishing pole from a yardstick, meterstick, or dowel rod. Attach a magnet to one end of the pole with a long piece of string. Cut out several construction paper fish. Draw a shape (or color, number, alphabet letter, etc.) on each fish and attach a paper clip. Place the fish in a cardboard box "pond" and invite your child to "go fishing." Make up games as you fish. Maybe you only want to catch the "star" fish, so all of the others have to be thrown back; maybe the triangle fish are pointy so you have be to extra careful when you throw them back; maybe the circle fish are good luck, so they earn you an extra turn!

 **(See page 2.)**

A Twist on Tic-Tac-Toe

Play tic-tac-toe with numbers to give your child practice with writing numbers. Draw a tic-tac-toe grid on a sheet of paper. Show your child how the game is played. Let him choose which symbol he will use. Then, take turns writing a 1 or a 4 in a space on the grid. A player who has three 1s or 4s in a horizontal, vertical, or diagonal line wins the game. Change the game by playing with different numbers. (See illustration.) Your child will get valuable practice recognizing and writing numbers from 1 to 9.

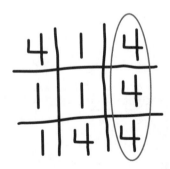

Piggy Bank Counting

Directions: With an adult, cut apart the piggy banks. Glue them onto the outside of snack-size resealable plastic bags. Then, count out the correct number of coins for each piggy bank. (Coins are provided on page 16.)

Circle Puzzles

Directions: Trace the clock and pizza with your finger and cut them out. With an adult, cut apart the puzzle pieces. Mix up each puzzle's pieces. Then, put the circle puzzles back together. For an added challenge, turn each puzzle's pieces over and try to put the circles back together without the pictures.

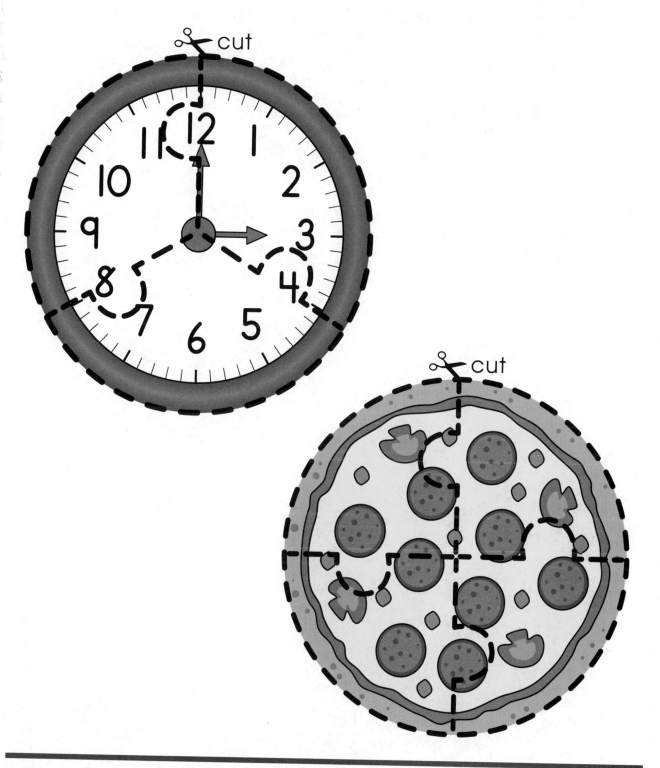

Let's Race

Directions: With an adult, cut apart the game cards on page 27. To play the game, place markers such as coins or buttons on *START*. Take turns drawing cards and moving your markers to the next matching color of triangle along the track. The first player to pass the *FINISH* banner wins the game.

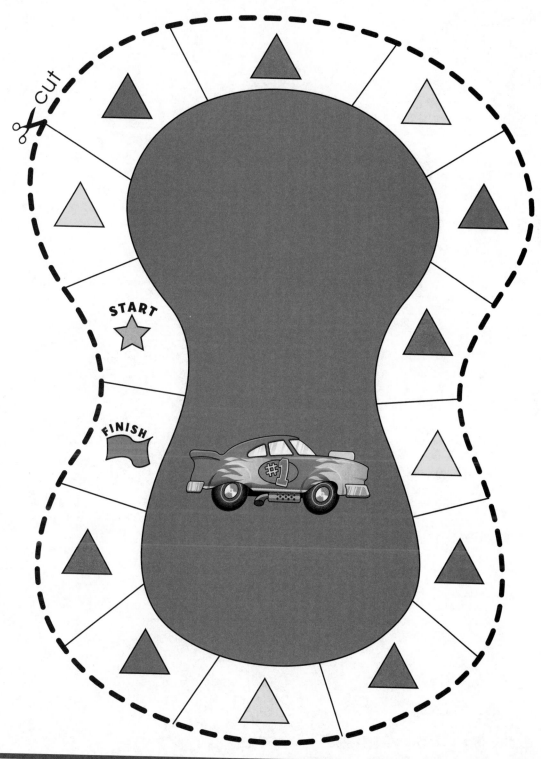

Directions: With an adult, cut apart the triangle game cards. Use them with the activity on page 25.

✂ cut

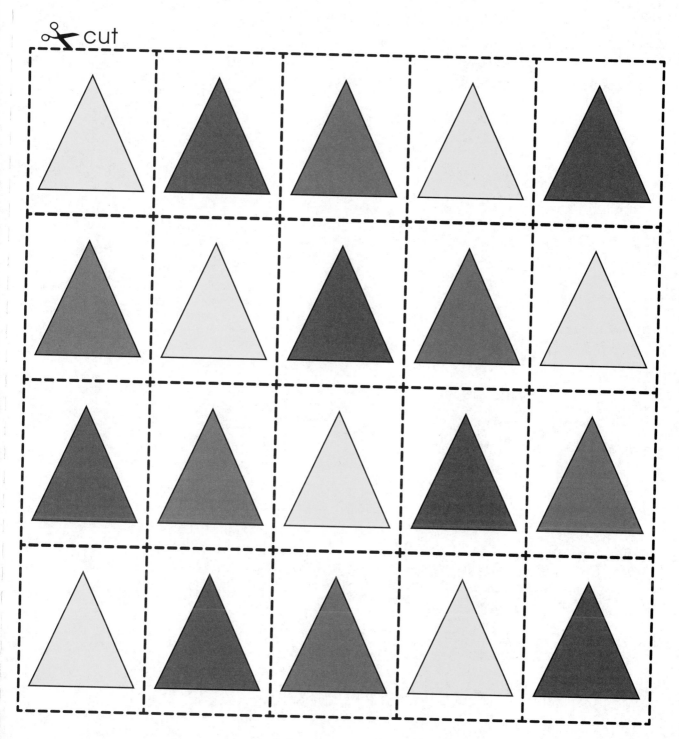

Ferris Wheel Shapes

Directions: Trace the rectangles below. Cut them out with the help of an adult. Match each rectangle with the same-sized rectangle in the picture.

cut

My Oval Owl

Directions: With an adult, cut out the ovals. Arrange the pieces to create an owl like the one shown. Glue the owl on a sheet of paper. Add the title "My Oval Owl."

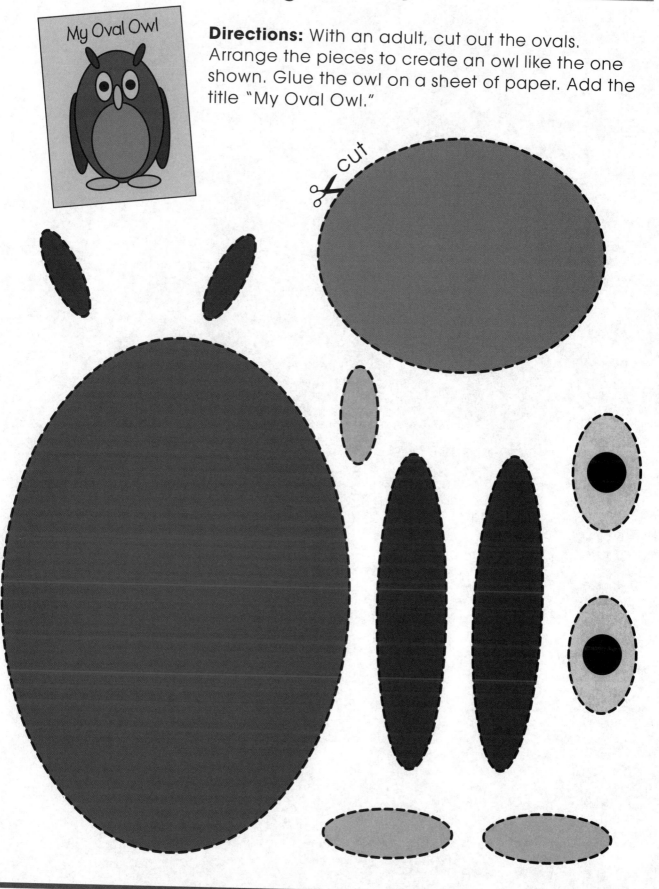

cut

Sailboat Shapes

Directions: Color the circle yellow. Color the rectangle blue. Color the triangle red. Cut out the shapes below. Match each shape to the same shape in the picture.

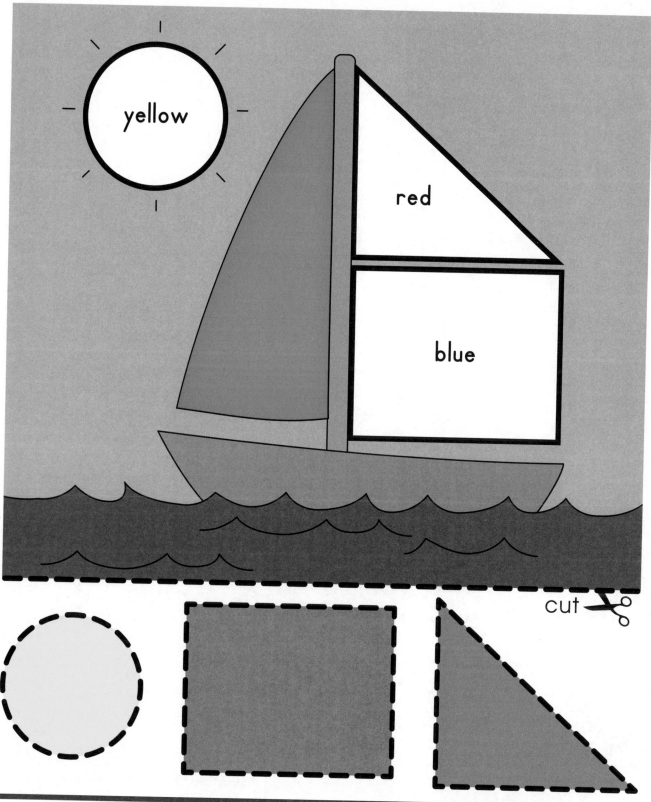

Directions: Color and cut out each shape below. Match it to the shape that is the same in the picture.

cut

blue

brown

purple

black

Directions: Color the triangles green. Color the square brown. With an adult, cut out the shapes. Use the shapes to make a tree like the one in the picture. Glue your tree on a sheet of paper. Draw some animals and birds and color them.

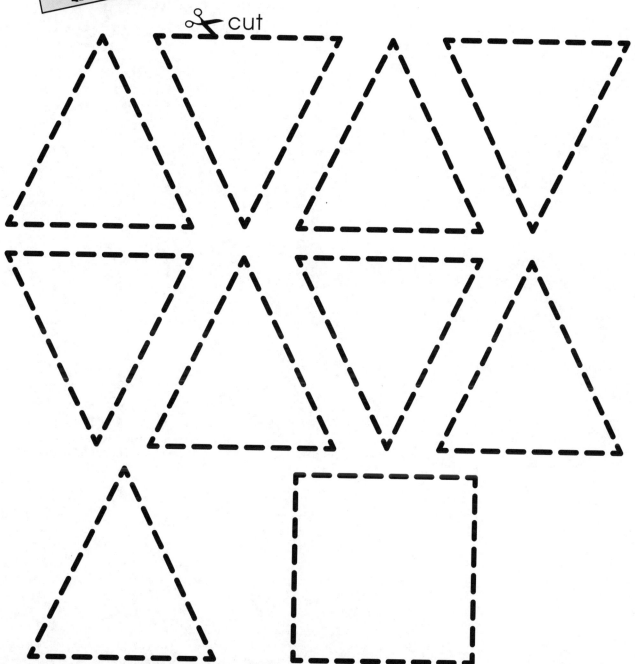

✂ cut

Rocket Shapes

Directions: With an adult, cut out the shapes under the rocket ship. Place them on the shapes in the picture that match. Then, use the shape pieces to make the rocket ship on a sheet of paper. Glue the rocket ship on the paper. Add a moon and stars to your picture.

cut

Shape Mobile

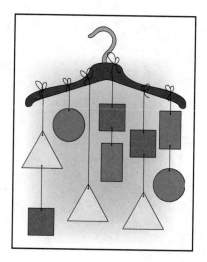

Directions: Cut out the shape patterns. Trace each shape four times on construction paper. Cut the shapes out. With an adult, punch a hole near the top of each shape. Attach different lengths of ribbon or yarn to the shapes. Hang them from a plastic clothes hanger. (See illustration.) Display the mobile in your room and use it to practice naming shapes.

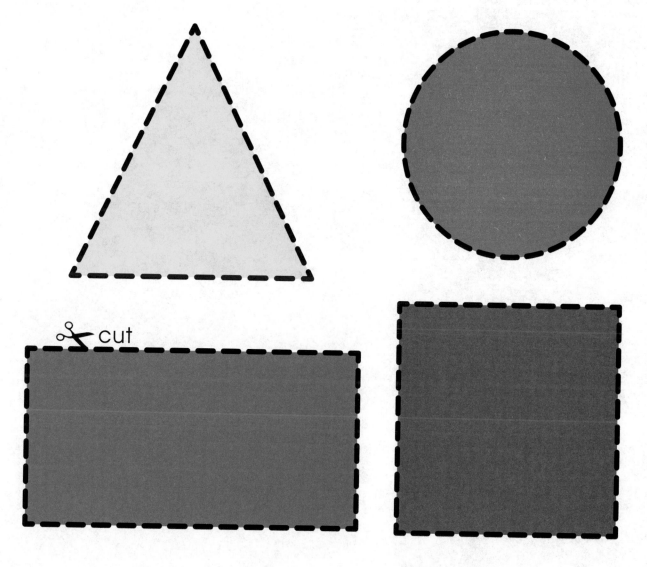

cut

Shape Puzzle

Directions: Cut out the grid and shape cards. Place the shape cards on the grid so that each row and each column has one of each shape. Turn the puzzle upside down and do it again.

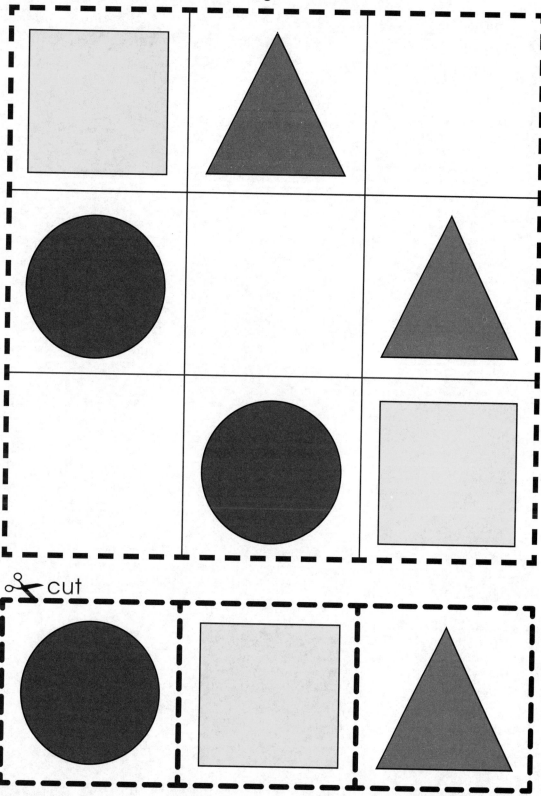

✂ cut

What's Missing?

Directions: Cut out the grid and shape cards. Place the shape cards on the grid so that each row and each column has one of each shape. Turn the puzzle upside down and do it again.

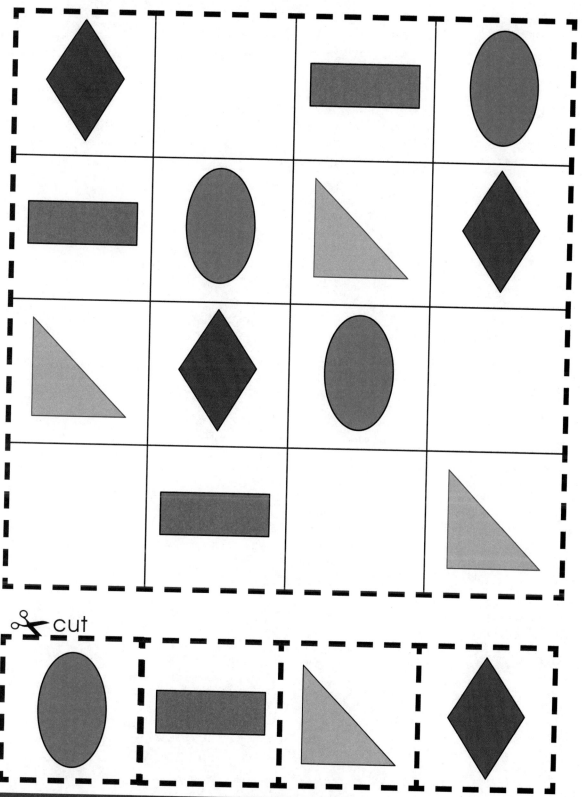

✂ cut

What's Missing?

Directions: Cut out the grid and shape cards. Place the shape cards on the grid so that each row and each column has one of each shape. Turn the puzzle upside down and do it again.

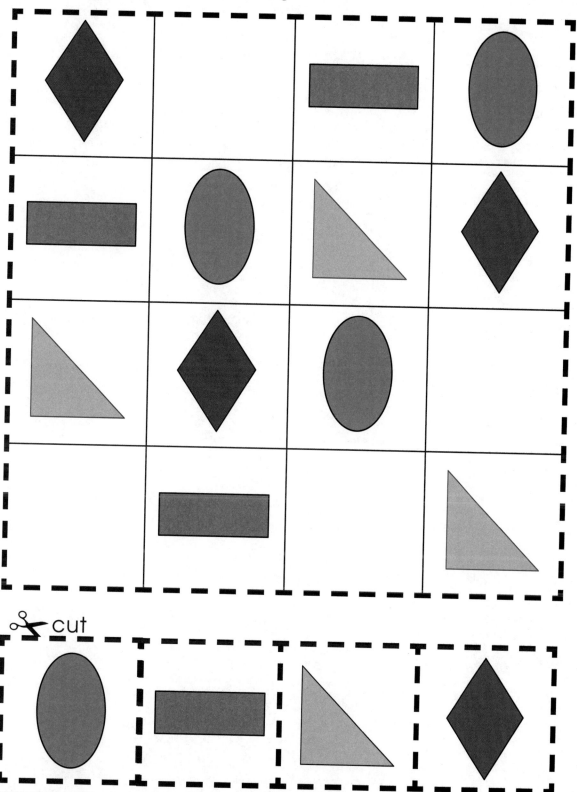

✂ cut

Big Elephant, Little Mouse

Directions: Cut apart the pictures at the bottom of the page. Name each picture. Place the objects that are little in real life next to the mouse. Place the objects that are big in real life next to the elephant.

cut

Little Fish, Big Whale

Directions: Cut apart the pictures at the bottom of the page. Name each picture. Place the objects that are little in real life next to the fish. Place the objects that are big in real life next to the whale.

✂ cut

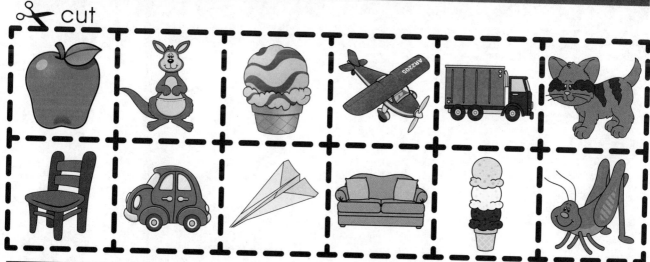

Animal Sports

Directions: Cut apart the three sets of cards. Arrange each set of pictures in order from the shortest to the tallest animals.

cut

Animals' Garden

Directions: Cut apart the three sets of cards. Look at the length of the objects the animals are holding. Arrange each set of pictures in order from the shortest to the longest objects.

cut ✂

Enough to Drink

Directions: Cut apart the pictures at the bottom of the page. Compare the amounts in the pitchers, cups, and bottles. Place the pictures with less on the left of the containers and the pictures with more on the right.

cut

Sorting Sea Creatures

Directions: Use a blue crayon to color two resealable plastic bags so that they look like aquariums with water. Glue the bags on the inside of a file folder. With an adult, label one bag *More* and the other bag *Less*. Cut apart the ocean creature cards. Then, sort the sets with more sea creatures into the *More* aquarium and the groups with less sea creatures into the *Less* aquarium.

✂ cut

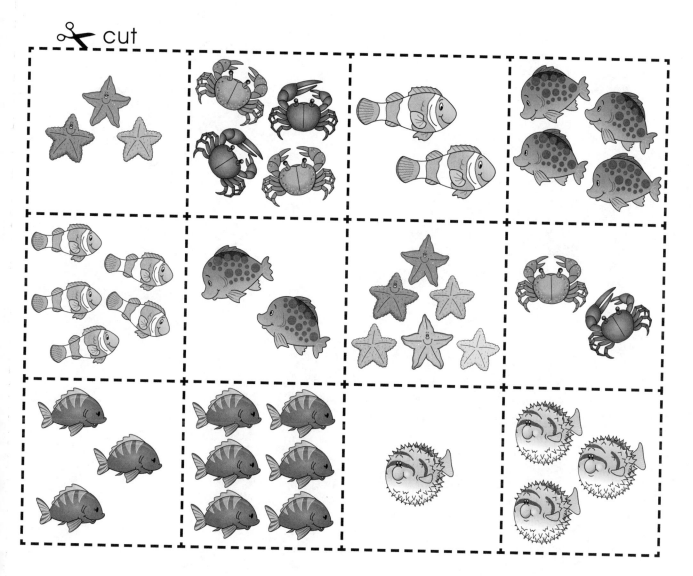

Feeding the Animals

Directions: Cut apart the cards. Arrange the pictures in each group in order from the animal that has the least to eat to the animal that has the most.

✂ cut

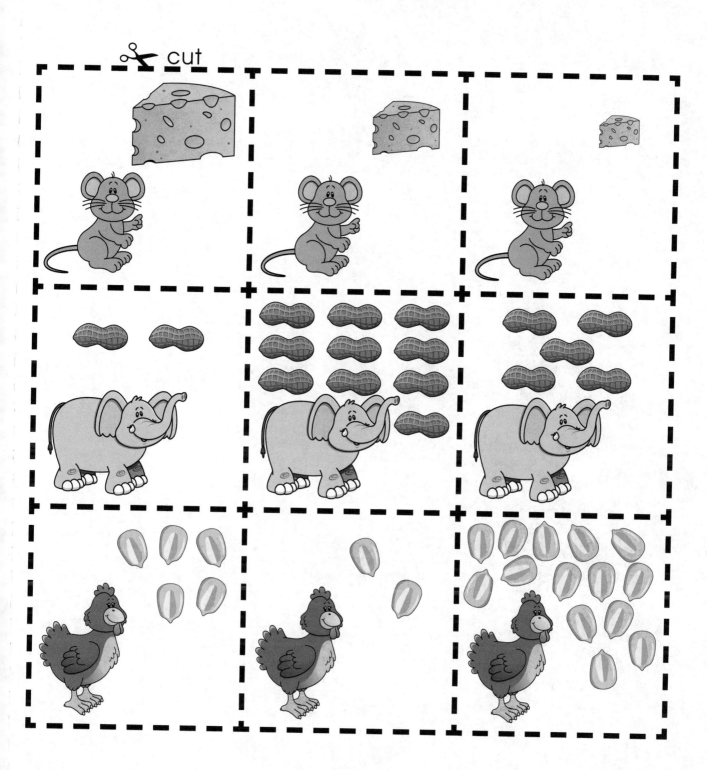

All by Myself

Directions: Cut apart the pictures. Arrange them in order from the event that happens first to the event that happens last. When you are finished, tell the stories aloud.

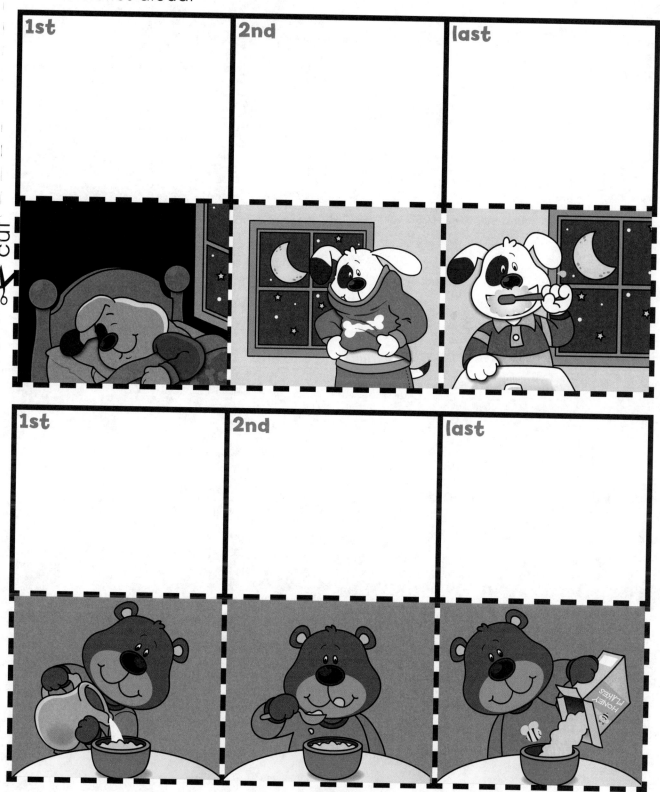

Things I Like to Do

Directions: Cut apart the pictures. Arrange them on the page in the correct order. When you are finished, tell the stories aloud.

Sometimes I Need Help

Directions: Cut apart the pictures. Arrange them on the page in the correct order. When you are finished, tell the story aloud.

3rd	1st
4th	2nd

✂ cut

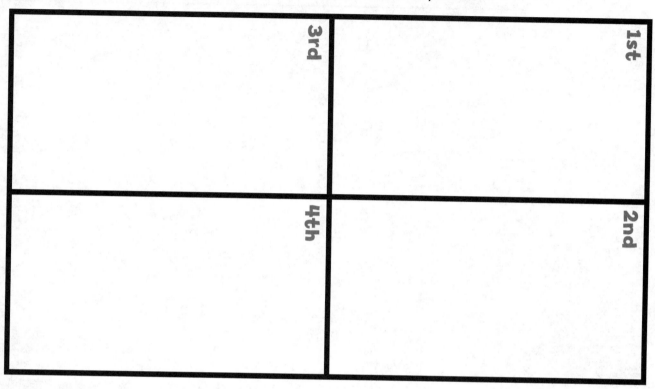

Directions: Cut apart the pictures. Arrange them on the page in the correct order. When you are finished, tell the story aloud.

1st	2nd
3rd	**4th**
5th	**6th**

✂ cut

Crossing the Street

Directions: Cut apart the pictures. Arrange them on the page in the correct order. When you are finished, tell the story aloud.

1st	2nd	3rd
4th	**5th**	**6th**

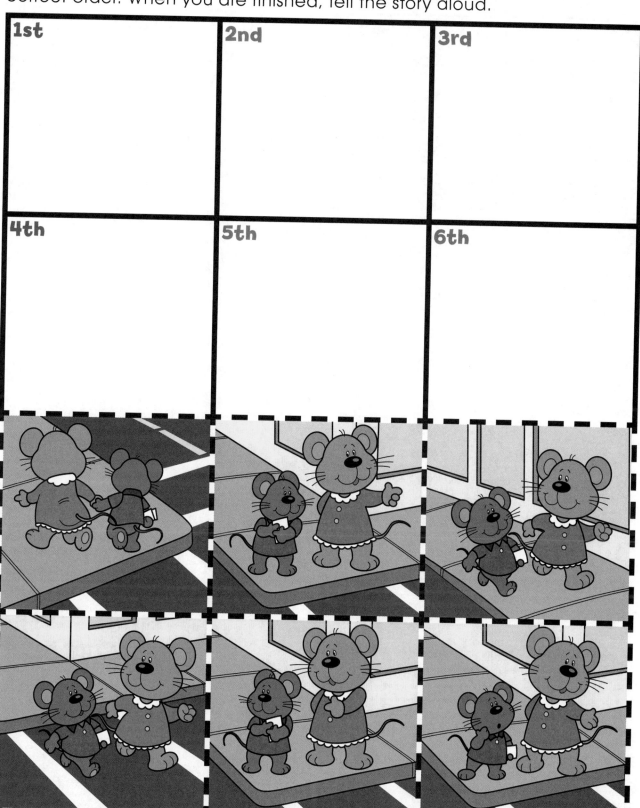

✂ cut

Shape Patterns

Directions: Cut apart the shape pattern cards. Place the shapes that continue each pattern in the box. Say the shapes in each pattern.

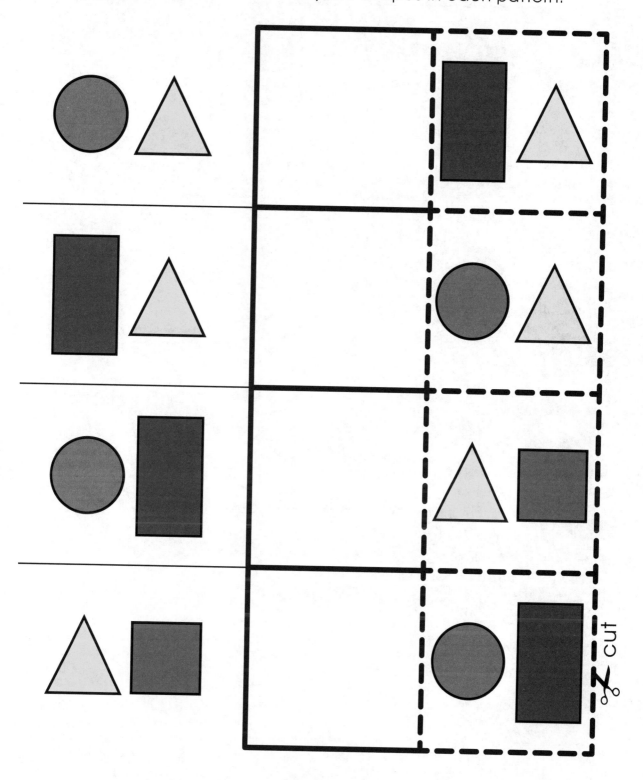

Squirrel Patterns

Directions: Cut apart the pictures at the bottom of the page. Arrange the pictures to continue the pattern in each row. Then, make your own patterns.

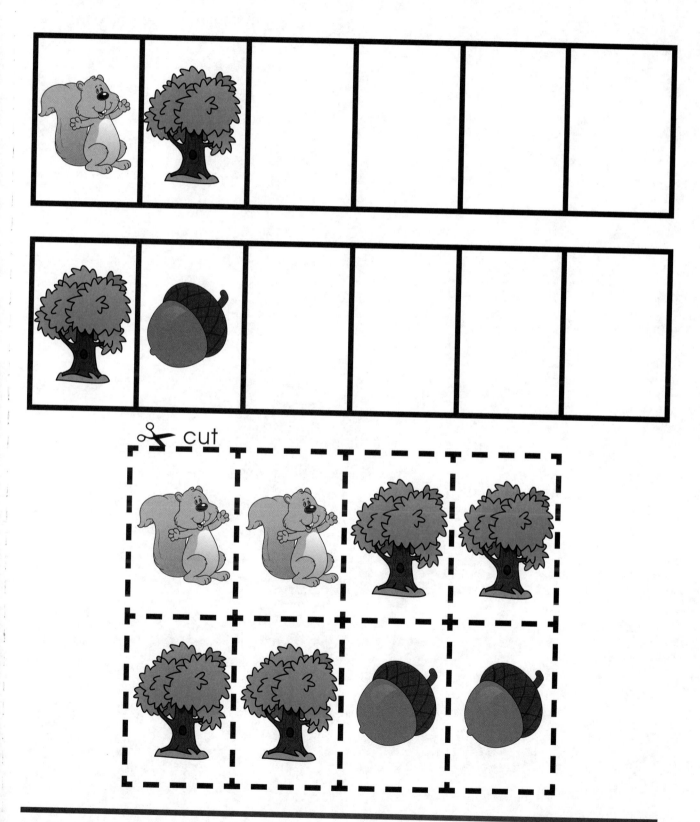

More Pattern Play

Directions: Cut apart the pattern cards. At the end of each row, place the cards that come next in the pattern.

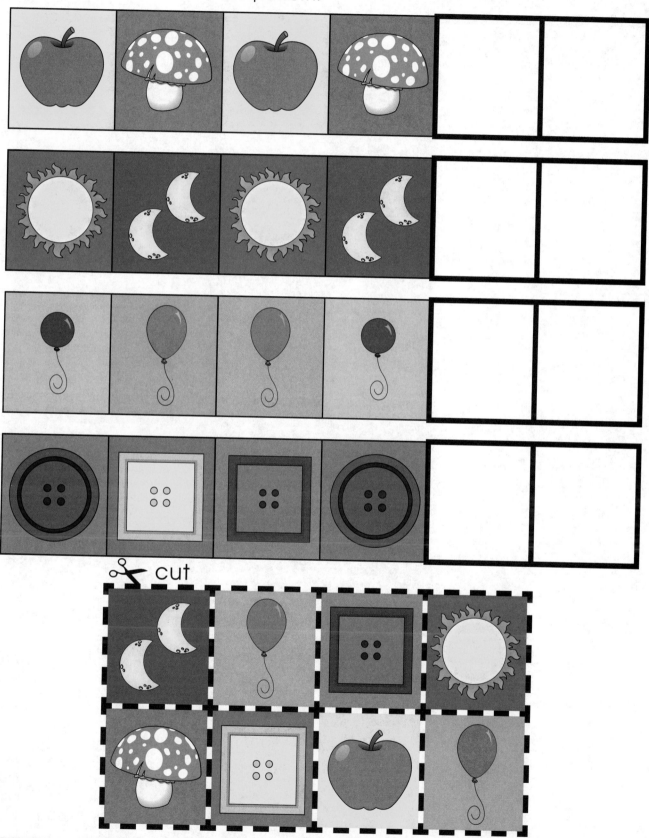

Terrific T-shirts

Directions: Cut apart the pictures at the bottom of the page. At the end of each row, place the picture that comes next in the pattern.

My Own Patterns

Directions: Cut apart the pattern cards. Use them to make your own patterns. Use these examples to get started.

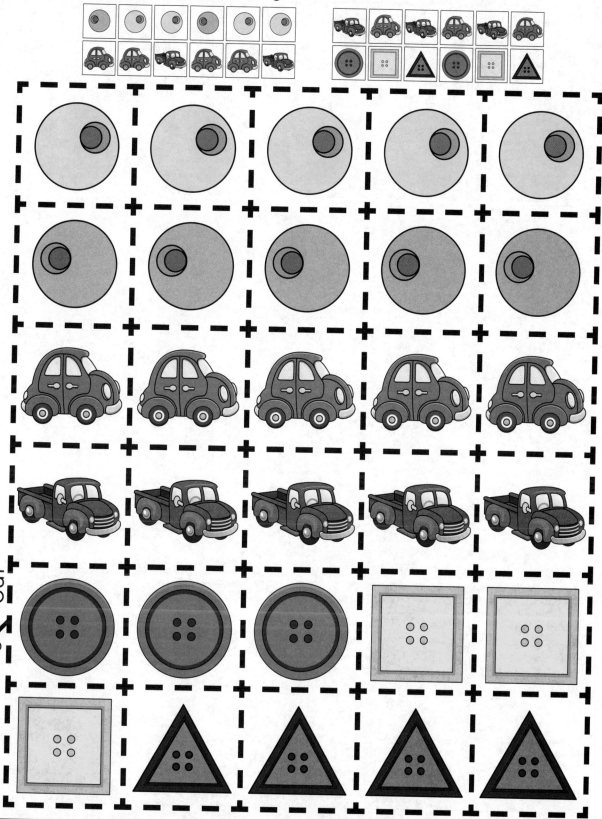